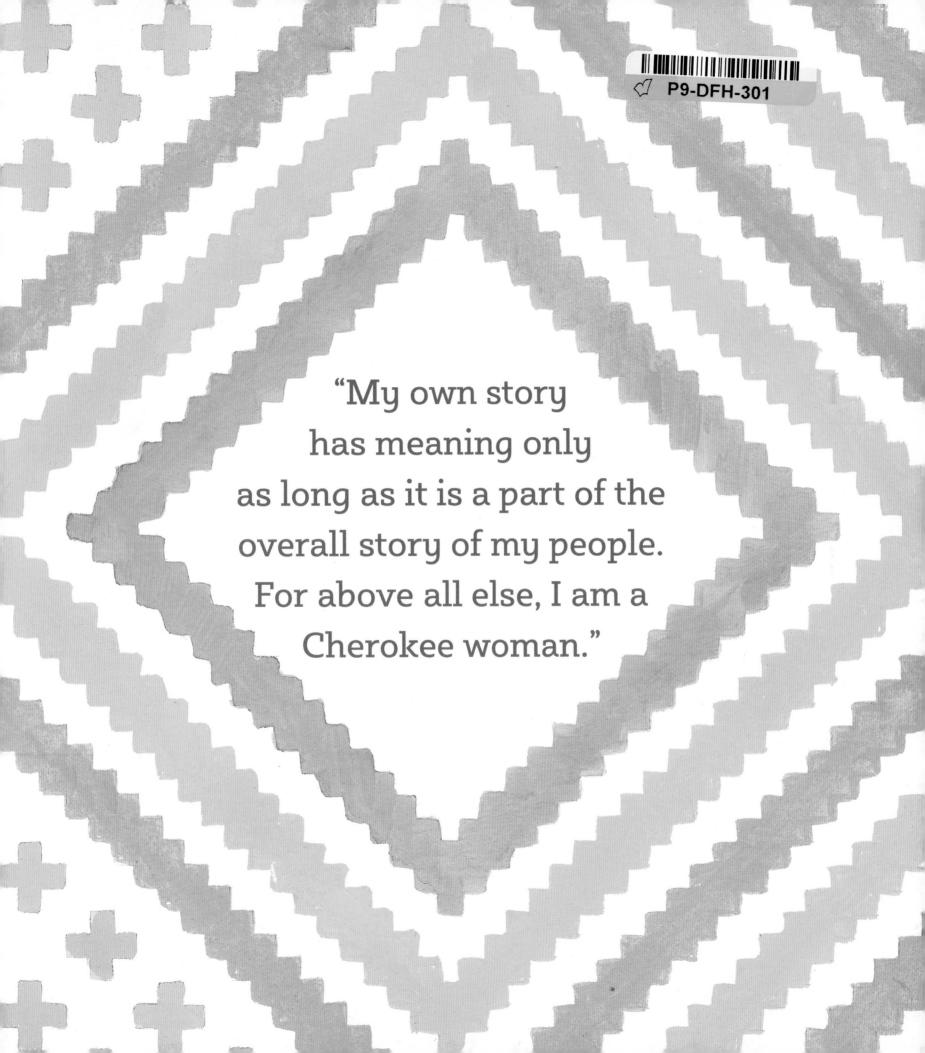

"My own story
has meaning only
as long as it is a part of the
overall story of my people.
For above all else, I am a
Cherokee woman."

For Arlo, Ava, Henry, Ilan, Isabel, Lilah, Mason, Nicole, Paloma,
Trixie, Violet, Willa, the next generation of leaders

—D.R.

To Rick, my loving husband of over fifty years, who has
always encouraged me to reach for my dreams

—L.K.

First Edition, February 2019
10 9 8 7 6 5 4 3 2 1
FAC-029191-18362

Printed in Malaysia

This book is set in 17-pt Adobe Garamond Pro/Fontspring; Eirlys, Sybilla Pro / Fontspring

Library of Congress Cataloging-in-Publication Data

Names: Rappaport, Doreen, author. • Kukuk, Linda, illustrator.
Title: Wilma's way home : the life of Wilma Mankiller / by Doreen Rappaport ; illustrated by Linda Kukuk. • Other titles: Life of Wilma Mankiller
• Description: First edition. • Los Angeles : Disney HYPERION, [2019] • Audience: Ages 6-8. • Identifiers: LCCN 2017056157 • ISBN 9781484747186 (hardcover)
• ISBN 1484747186 (hardcover) • Subjects: LCSH: Mankiller, Wilma Pearl, 1945-2010—Juvenile literature. • Cherokee women—Biography—Juvenile literature.
• Cherokee Indians—Kings and rulers—Biography—Juvenile literature. • Cherokee Nation, Oklahoma—Juvenile literature. • Classification: LCC E99.C5 R27 2019
• DDC 973.04/975570092 [B]—dc23
LC record available at https://lccn.loc.gov/2017056157

Reinforced binding
Visit www.DisneyBooks.com

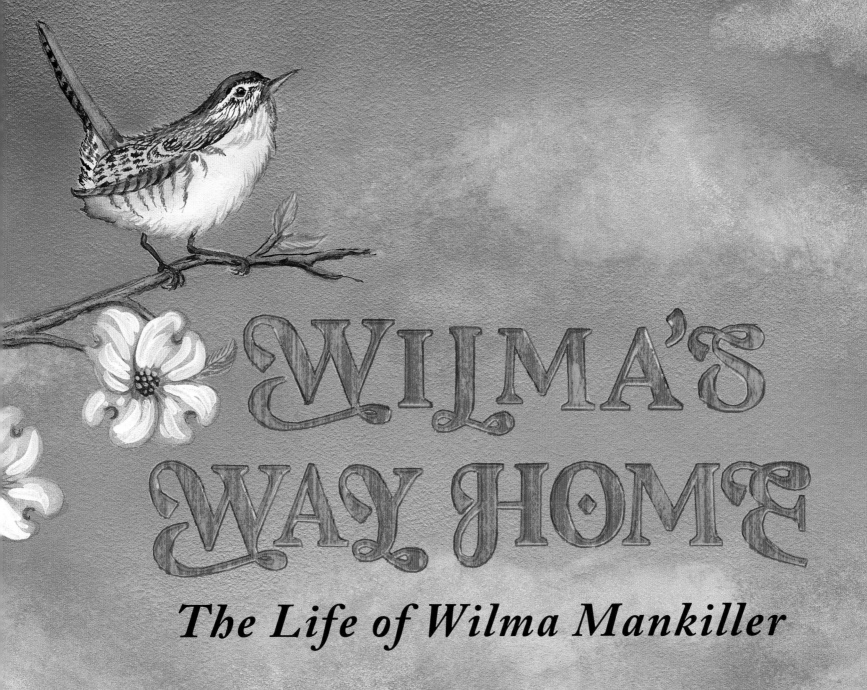

WILMA'S WAY HOME

The Life of Wilma Mankiller

BY DOREEN RAPPAPORT

ILLUSTRATED BY LINDA KUKUK

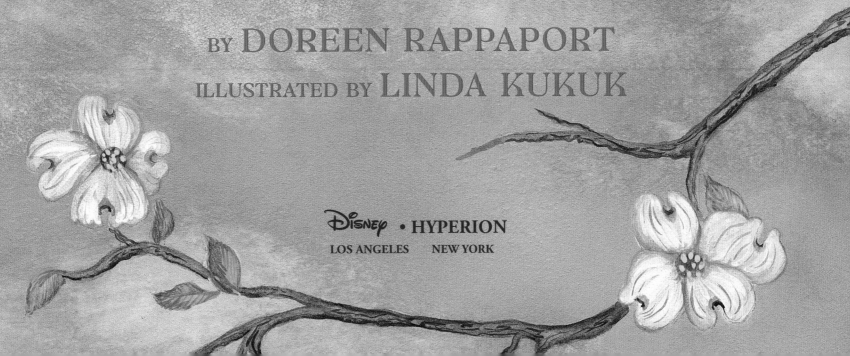

Disney • HYPERION

LOS ANGELES   NEW YORK

Full-time jobs for Cherokee people
were scarce in rural Oklahoma.
Wilma's family cut and peeled wood for railroad ties.
They picked beans and grew strawberries.
Wilma hauled water from the spring
that her family drank from and
used to cool fresh milk and butter.
But no matter how hard they worked,
they couldn't earn enough money
for their family of eleven.

Few homes in rural Oklahoma
had plumbing or electricity.
Wilma's mother cooked on a wood-burning stove
that also heated the house her father built.

Like rural families everywhere
who could not find work,
the Mankillers raised vegetables and
hunted and fished to put food on the table.

**"It was a hard life.
We were really poor—
'dirt poor' is how they say it in Oklahoma."**

Wilma's mother, Irene, was of Dutch Irish descent.
Her parents disapproved of Charley Mankiller,
because he was older and Native.
But Wilma's parents loved each other so much
they got married anyway.

Wilma's mother taught her
the names of trees and flowers.
Wilma spent many days outdoors,
especially when the dogwood trees
were in bloom.

**"My father must have known somehow
that I would love flowers,
because the Cherokee name he gave me,
'Atsilvsgi,' means flower."**

Wilma spent her nights reading books and
playing Chinese checkers carved by her father.
He was a great reader and storyteller and
passed his love of both to his children.

**"The warmth and love in our family
made up for the lack of material things."**

Wilma's family was rich
in love and community.
Cherokee people survived
through *Gadugi*, the philosophy of helping each other.
Families who raised chickens
swapped eggs for milk.
People traded homegrown vegetables
for store-bought goods.

**"We are all interdependent.
Do things for others,
rather than just for yourself."**

At get-togethers,
the grown-ups talked and played cards.
The children played hide-and-seek
and kick the can.
They caught fireflies,
put them in jars,
watched them flash on and off, then let them go.

At the *gatiyo*,
the ceremonial Stomp Dance grounds,
Wilma felt part
of the ancient religious songs and dances.

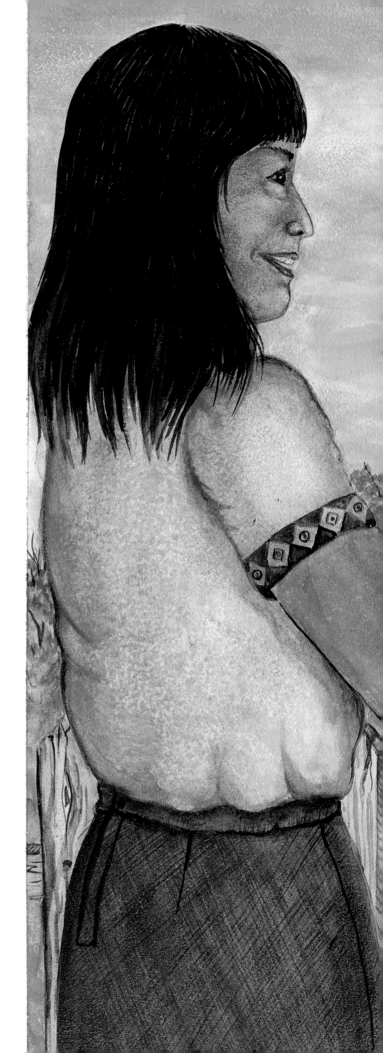

When Wilma was almost eleven,
the federal government created a new policy
to relocate Indians from their land to cities,
promising good jobs and better housing.

Wilma's father did not want to move.
He remembered all the times
the federal government forced
Native people off their homelands.

In 1838, at gunpoint, government soldiers
forced Cherokee men, women, and children
to leave their homelands
in the Carolinas and Georgia.
They were marched a thousand miles west
in the freezing winter and sweltering summer.
Many were whipped along the way.
Disease and starvation struck.
More than four thousand Cherokees died
on this forced removal west,
which Wilma's father referred to as
anitsalagi, dodigegatinvstanv—
"All Cherokees, they were brought on the trail."
Most history books refer
to this tragic event
as the Trail of Tears.

Wilma's father saw relocation
as one more way to separate
Indians from their people
and to destroy their culture.
But he was finding it impossible
to get work in Oklahoma.
Perhaps city life would give his children
a better future.

Wilma did not want to leave her home.

**"I cried for days, not unlike the children
who had stumbled down the
Trail of Tears. . . ."**

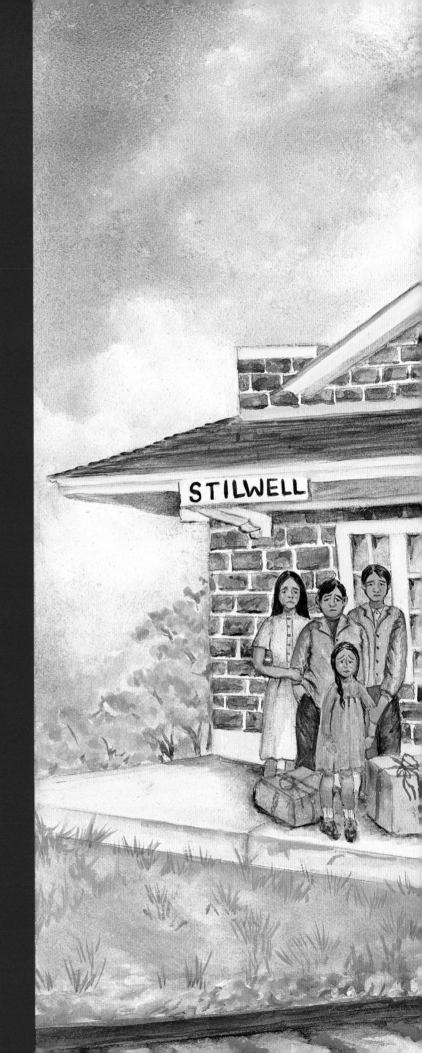

Life in San Francisco, California,
shocked Wilma.
No more fragrant dogwood blooms.
No more flowering trees.
No more hills and green valleys.
Only buildings close together and
some people sleeping in the streets.
Instead of starlit skies,
glaring neon lights.
No more singing wrens.
Only blaring sirens and car horns.

**"One day I was here, and the next day
I was trying to deal with the mysteries of
television, indoor plumbing, neon lights,
and elevators."**

There were no better jobs
and no better housing.
The family missed their friends and relatives.

At school when the teacher called the roll,
Wilma's classmates laughed at her name,
and she wished she could disappear.
But her parents told her to be proud of her name.
The family was given this name
because in the early days
they guarded village homes.
When enemies attacked,
these warriors fought back.

Wilma's classmates mocked her clothing
and her Oklahoma accent.
She tried to lose her accent but couldn't.

**"It was not that I was so much poorer
than the others,
but I was definitely
from another culture."**

Seeking community, the family went
to the Indian Center in San Francisco.
Her father worked to open
a free health clinic for Indians.
The family met other Native people
who also longed to return to their homelands.
All agreed this federal policy was a disaster.

**"It robbed us of our vitality
and sense of place."**

Wilma hated city life.
She kept running away to
her maternal grandmother, who lived
on a farm eighty-one miles away.
Finally her parents sent her to live there.

**"The hard work and fresh air were so good.
The year on the farm
was just what I needed."**

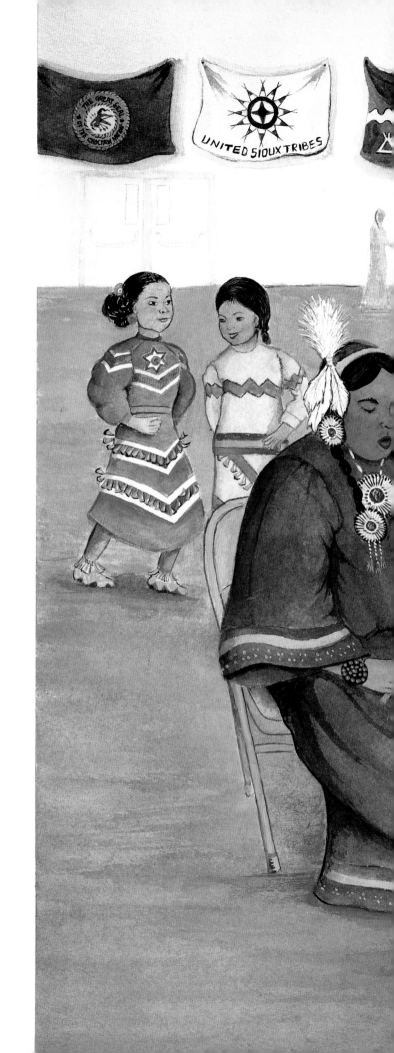

Wilma married at eighteen.
Within two years she was
the mother of two girls.

It was the 1960s, an era of protests.
Black Americans marched for equality.
Latino farmworkers went on strike for better wages.
Young and old demonstrated against war.
Women met in groups to talk about their lives.
Native people protested the taking of tribal lands.

**"I began to have dreams
about more freedom and independence."**

Wilma started college.
She went back to the Indian Center
and shared her life with other Indians.
Her husband was not pleased
with her new interests and friends.

**"Hugo expected me to step completely away
from the Indian Center and
from my birth family."**

Starting in November 1969,
hundreds of indigenous people
took over Alcatraz Island,
a former prison in San Francisco Bay.
They claimed it for "Indians of All Tribes."
Four of Wilma's siblings were among the occupiers.
Wilma visited often and helped raise money.

Reporters visited and listened and learned
about the five hundred years
of government abuse of Native people.
They wrote about the many broken treaties, and
non-Native Americans were reminded that
the entire country was once Indian land
before it was taken away.

**"It was life changing. It was the first time
I saw Native people stand up and say we
will hold this island until people notice us.
Before I had a lot of feelings and didn't
know how to articulate them or
frame them."**

After nineteen months, government police
forcibly removed the protestors, but
their struggle for their rights continued.

Wilma got a job at the Oakland Indian Center
working with children.
When she needed support or money for projects,
she turned to Native people,
and they always helped.

She took her daughters to visit
tribal communities in California.
They ate traditional foods,
attended traditional dances,
and listened to traditional stories.

**"The militants, the wise elders,
the keepers of the medicine,
the storytellers—were my best teachers.
I felt like a newborn
whose eyes have just opened to the first light."**

Her path ahead became clear.

Wilma separated from her husband
and returned with her daughters
to Oklahoma,
to the familiar hills and trees
and the voices of wrens and mockingbirds.

She attended the sacred ceremonies
and built a home on her ancestral land.
She made new friends and
reached out to old ones.
Her father died.
Her mother and nine of her siblings
moved back, too.

Cherokee Chief Ross Swimmer
hired Wilma to work
for the Cherokee Nation government.
When he saw how hard she worked,
he gave her more responsibility.
She went back to finish college.

**"I felt whole again for the first time
since my childhood."**

Two years later, Wilma almost died
in a car accident.
Her sister Linda cared for her
through seventeen operations.

Wilma faced many more illnesses, and
each time family and friends helped her.
Her brother and niece donated
their kidneys to save her life.

**"During the long healing process,
I fell back on what elders call
'a Cherokee approach' to life—
to think positively,
to take what is handed out
and turn it into a better path."**

Eighteen months later, Wilma returned to work.
Chief Swimmer asked her to develop
new projects in rural Cherokee communities.

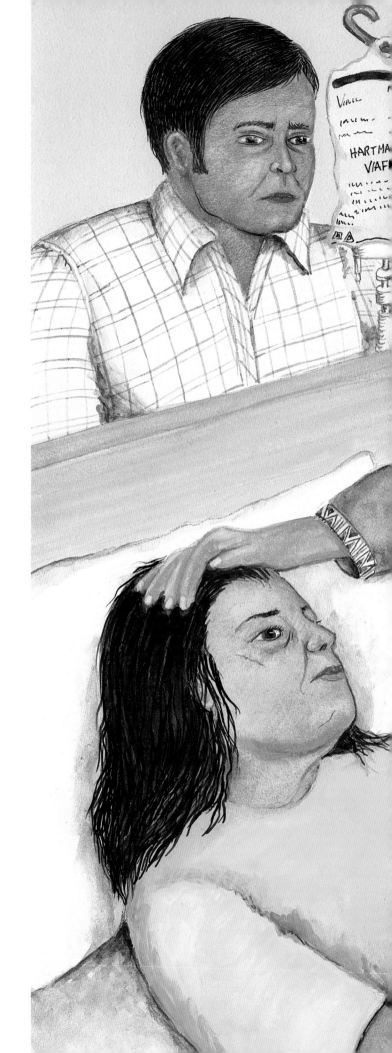

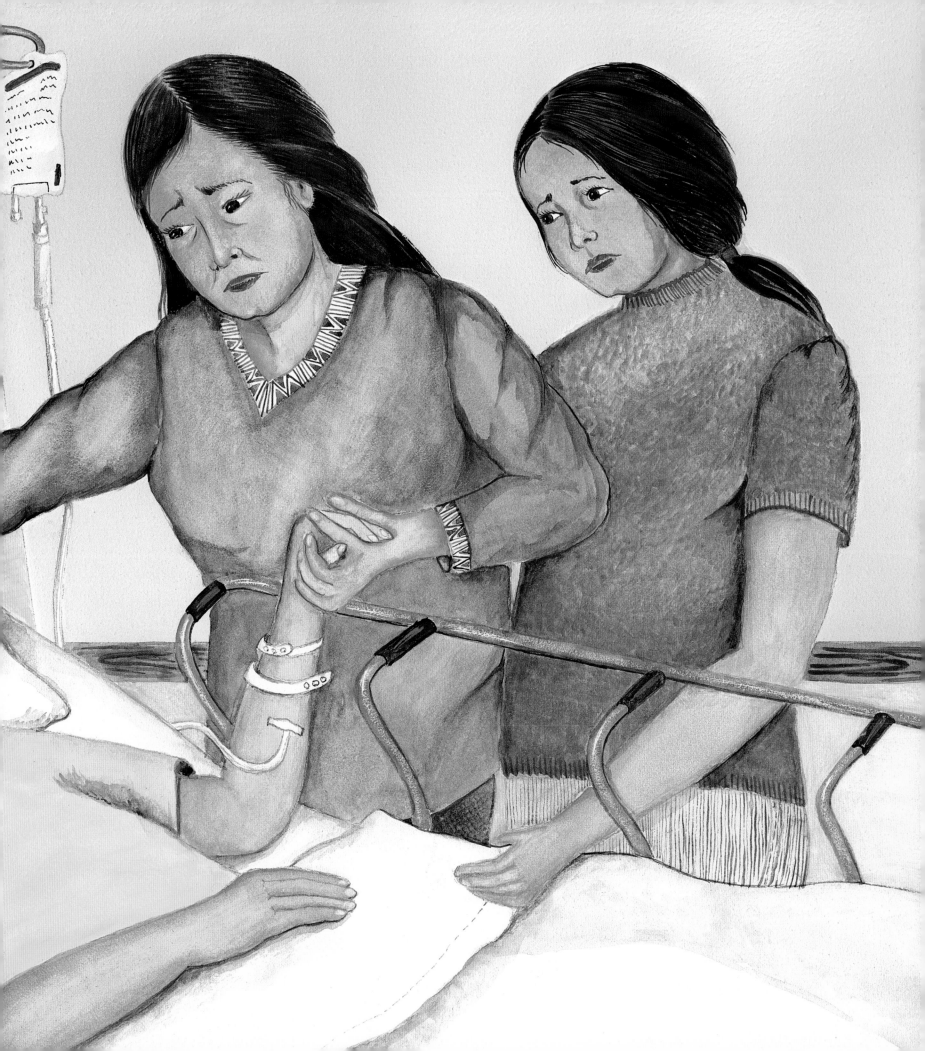

Wilma and co-organizer Charlie Soap
went to Bell, a community of 350 people.
Jobs there were few. Homes were run down.
Almost no houses had running water.

Wilma saw that in Bell,
as in her community,
these Cherokee people had survived
through *Gadugi*, by helping each other.
Those who fished shared their catch.
Hunters shared their meat.
Young people cut wood to heat elders' homes.

Wilma and Charlie believed that
the Cherokee people of Bell knew best
what they needed to do to better their lives.
For a year they met with them
and listened to them
map out what they should do first.
The Cherokees wanted running water.

**"I had an abiding faith
in the ability of Cherokee people
to solve their own problems."**

Wilma applied for grants to fund the project.
The community worked in teams,
mapping out the route of the waterline,
digging trenches through flint rock and clay,
and lugging pipes into ditches to be buried.
Team after team, week after week,
for twenty-one months,
until the pipeline
brought water to eighty-one homes.

There was no grant money for plumbing
for the non-Cherokees in Bell, so
their Cherokee neighbors raised it.

The Cherokees of Bell began to believe
that they had the power to change their lives.
They repaired their homes,
built twenty-five new houses
and a community center.

**"The waterline and the houses are
more than just projects.
They are symbols of renewal."**

This tiny community inspired others
around the world to help themselves
improve their lives.

Chief Swimmer asked Wilma
to run with him in the 1983 election.
Before the Europeans came,
Cherokee women and men shared political power.
But European ways influenced the Cherokees
and limited the political role of women.
Now some Cherokees believed other tribes
would laugh if a woman was elected.

Wilma received hate mail.
Her car tires were slashed.
At first, few people came to her rallies.
Wilma visited people in the seven thousand square miles
of the fourteen counties of the Cherokee Nation.
She answered their questions
and told them what she believed in.
Family, friends, and Charlie Soap
helped her campaign.
It was a tough race, but she won.

**"In my household, no one ever said to me,
'you can't do this because
you're a woman, Indian, or poor.'
Of course I would not have listened to them
if they had tried."**

Most men on the tribal council
did not support her.
But Wilma forged ahead,
creating programs to better
the economic lives of her people.

In 1985 Chief Swimmer left
to work in Washington, and
Wilma became principal chief.
Two years later she ran on her own
and became the first woman chief
of the Cherokee Nation,
the second largest Indian nation
in the United States.
The third time she ran
she was reelected in a landslide.

**"Prior to my election, young Cherokee girls
would never have thought
that they might grow up to be chief."**

Wilma found personal happiness, too.
Her work relationship with Charlie Soap
had turned into love,
and they married.

During Wilma's ten years of leadership,
the Cherokee Nation revived a tribal high school,
built four health clinics, two day-care centers,
and a job corps training center.
New businesses—a cattle and poultry ranch,
gift shops, and a motel—were created,
bringing pride to her people,
along with millions of dollars
to better their lives.

Wilma's work brought world attention
to the Cherokee Nation and to Wilma,
and pride to all Native peoples.

Unfortunately her many illnesses
led to her early death at sixty-four.
But her vision and accomplishments
remain a model of how leaders should lead
and how all people can empower themselves.

**"Women can help turn the world right
side up. We bring a more collaborative
approach to government."**

AUTHOR'S NOTE

When Americans were asked to suggest women to be put on the twenty-dollar bill, one of my top votes was for Wilma Mankiller. Wilma Mankiller represents the best of what a leader can be—she respected people and trusted that, regardless of their economic circumstances, they were capable of solving their problems and figuring out what needed to be done to change and better their lives. Instead of imposing her wishes upon the residents of Bell, Wilma and her coworker—and later husband—Charlie Soap spent a year listening to the Cherokee people there discuss what project should be tackled first to better their living conditions. When Wilma later became chief, she continued helping people empower themselves.

I had the privilege of going to Oklahoma and meeting with Michael Wallis, who coauthored Wilma's autobiography, Charlie Soap, and Wilma's dear friend Kristina Kiehl. All three shared their personal memories of this extraordinary woman and answered many questions as I moved from draft to draft. Charlie brought me into the home he shared with Wilma, took me to the site of her school, and drove me around the area so I could get a feel for the sky and the green and the trees. He read the manuscript, made suggestions and corrections, and generously shared the Cherokee words in this book, helping to create the pronunciation guide. I thank Yvonne Wakim Dennis and Arlene Hirschfelder for their reading and critique of my early draft. Wilma Mankiller's struggles, her triumphs, her whole being have inspired me. I hope she inspires you.
—Doreen Rappaport

ILLUSTRATOR'S NOTE

Having always lived in Oklahoma and being of Native American ancestry, I naturally had heard about Wilma Mankiller and her accomplishments as chief of the Cherokee Nation. However, when I found out I would be illustrating a book on her life, I began my journey to get to know her on a more personal level. I read her autobiography, traveled to northeastern Oklahoma to visit with her husband in their home on Mankiller Flats, and spoke with any relative or friend I could find. I wanted to make sure my illustrations reflected her true spirit. Without fail, every person I spoke with who had known Wilma thought of themselves as her "best" friend. To me, that shows the warmth of character she possessed.

While researching, sketching, and painting, I asked God to help me do her justice, and I asked Wilma to help me get it right. Both came through for me. I could feel Wilma's spirit with me every step of the way. For example, when I was having trouble coming up with the scene for the end of her life, I went to sleep one night and dreamed the image that I would ultimately paint. That scene was an Oklahoma sunset with Wilma wrapped in the Cherokee Nation flag of her people. However, when it came time to paint that scene, I was struggling to make it like the image I had dreamed. After several failed attempts, I got up one morning and asked God and Wilma for help. I said, "You have given me this beautiful vision, please help me do this right." I took out my board, and almost effortlessly my vision became reality.

I think Wilma's vision was to help her people in any way she could. I believe her life, despite her own struggles, became that reality.
—Linda Kukuk

IMPORTANT EVENTS

Nov. 18, 1945 Wilma Pearl Mankiller is born in Tahlequah, Oklahoma, the sixth of eleven children of Charley and Clara Irene Sitton Mankiller.

1956 The federal government moves Mankiller's family off their land in Oklahoma to San Francisco, California, as part of the Bureau of Indian Affairs relocation program.

1963 Eighteen-year-old Wilma marries Hector Hugo Olaya de Bardi.

1964 Her daughter Felicia Olaya is born; two years later Gina Olaya is born.

1968 AIM, the American Indian Movement, is formed in Minneapolis, Minnesota. Members stage demonstrations and sit-ins to protest the loss of tribal property and resources.

November 19, 1969–June 11, 1971 Native Americans occupy Alcatraz Island, citing an 1868 treaty that said all unused federal lands must return to Indian use.

February 20, 1971 Wilma's father, Charley Mankiller, dies, and is brought back to Oklahoma to be buried on his ancestral land.

1973–76 Wilma attends Skyline College and San Francisco State College, completing her degree at the University of Arkansas.

1974 She divorces her husband.

October 1977 Wilma becomes the community development director for the Cherokee Nation.

1979 Wilma survives a near-fatal auto accident.

1980 She is diagnosed with myasthenia gravis, a crippling disease of the voluntary muscles of the body.

January 1981 She founds and directs the community development department of the Cherokee Nation.

August 14, 1983 Mankiller becomes deputy chief of the Cherokee Nation and president of the tribal council. Ross Swimmer is the principal chief.

September 1985–1987 Swimmer becomes the assistant secretary of the interior of the US Bureau of Indian Affairs. Wilma succeeds him as the first female principal chief of the Cherokee Nation.

October 19, 1986 She marries Charlie Soap.

1987 She is elected principal chief in her own campaign.

1988 Wilma and other tribal leaders meet with President Ronald Reagan.

1991 Wilma wins her third election, receiving almost 83 percent of the vote. The fifteen-member Cherokee tribal council includes six women.

1994 Due to health considerations, Wilma does not seek reelection.

1996 She accepts a Montgomery Fellowship to teach at Dartmouth College.

1998 Wilma is awarded the Presidential Medal of Freedom by President Bill Clinton.

April 6, 2010 The Cherokee Nation announces Wilma Mankiller's death.

PRONUNCIATION GUIDE

Below is a phonetic guide to the four different Cherokee terms that are in the book. This guide was prepared by the Cherokee Language Program at Western Carolina University, Cullowhee, North Carolina, and by Charlie Soap in consultation with Cherokee elders. Syllables that are usually stressed are in caps. The guide approximates how these words sound.

Atsilvsgi (ah-jee-LUH-skee): flower.

Gadugi (gah-DOO-gee): the Cherokee philosophy of people helping each other.

gatiyo (gah-tee-yo): the ceremonial Stomp Dance grounds.

anitsalagi, dodigegatinvstanv (ah-knee-jah-lay-keh doh-dee-geh-gah-tee-nah-stah-nah): "All Cherokees, they were brought on the trail."

SELECTED BIBLIOGRAPHY

Bevier, Thomas. "They Made It Happen." *Parade Magazine,* February 10, 1985.

Fixico, Donald L. *The Urban Indian Experience in America.* Albuquerque: University of New Mexico Press, 2000.

Green, Rayna. *Women in American Indian Society.* New York: Chelsea House Publishers, 1992.

Hubbard, Julie. "Mankiller: Former Cherokee Chief Still Making a Difference." *News From Indian Country: The Independent Native Journal,* July 28, 2004.

Mankiller, Wilma and Wallis Michael. *Mankiller: A Chief and Her People.* New York: St. Martin's Press, 1994.

—— *Every Day Is a Good Day: Reflections by Contemporary Indigenous Women.* Golden, Colorado: Fulcrum Publishing, 2004.

"Q&A with Wilma Mankiller." *In the Field.* Chicago: Field Museum, May–June 1999.

Van Biema, David. "Activist Wilma Mankiller Is Set to Become the First Female Chief of the Cherokee Nation." *People,* December 2, 1985.

Verhovek, Sam Howe. "The Name's the Most and Least of Her." *New York Times,* November 4, 1993.

Whittemore, Hank. "She Leads a Nation." *Parade Magazine,* August 18, 1991.

LEARN MORE ABOUT WILMA MANKILLER AND THE CHEROKEE NATION

"A Modern Pioneer in the Cherokee Nation (Wilma Mankiller)"
https://www.youtube.com/watch?v=zqqkKrz5U5Y

Mankiller
www.mankillerdoc.com

The Cherokee Nation
www.cherokee.org

"The Cherokee Language"
https://www.youtube.com/watch?v=saSSlSQwlwg

The Cherokee Word for Water
www.cw4w.com

"The Cherokee Word for Water with Charlie Soap and Kristina Kiehl"
https://www.youtube.com/watch?v=WIdRekfqRfk

"Tom Belt: Cherokee Language Teacher"
https://vimeo.com/29736103

"Wilma Mankiller Memorial Video Part I Living a Good Life.mpg"
https://www.youtube.com/watch?v=HDG8Y38Is30

"Wilma Mankiller Reflects on Columbus Day"
https://www.npr.org/templates/story/story.php?storyId=95622629

SOURCE NOTES

In many instances, quotes by Wilma Mankiller have been shortened without changing their meaning. Punctuation has been simplified. The text begins on page 6. The quotes on the front endpapers and pages 6, 8 (top and bottom), 14, 18, 20 (top and bottom), 22 (top), 26, 30, 36, 38, and 40 come from *Mankiller: A Chief and Her People*. The quote on page 10 is from "She Leads a Nation." The quotes on pages 16 and 24 are from "Mankiller: Former Cherokee Chief Still Making a Difference." The quotes on pages 22 (bottom), 28, and 32 are from *Every Day Is a Good Day: Reflections by Contemporary Indigenous Women*. The quote on page 34 is from "They Made It Happen." The quote on the back endpapers is from "Activist Wilma Mankiller Is Set to Become the First Female Chief of the Cherokee Nation."

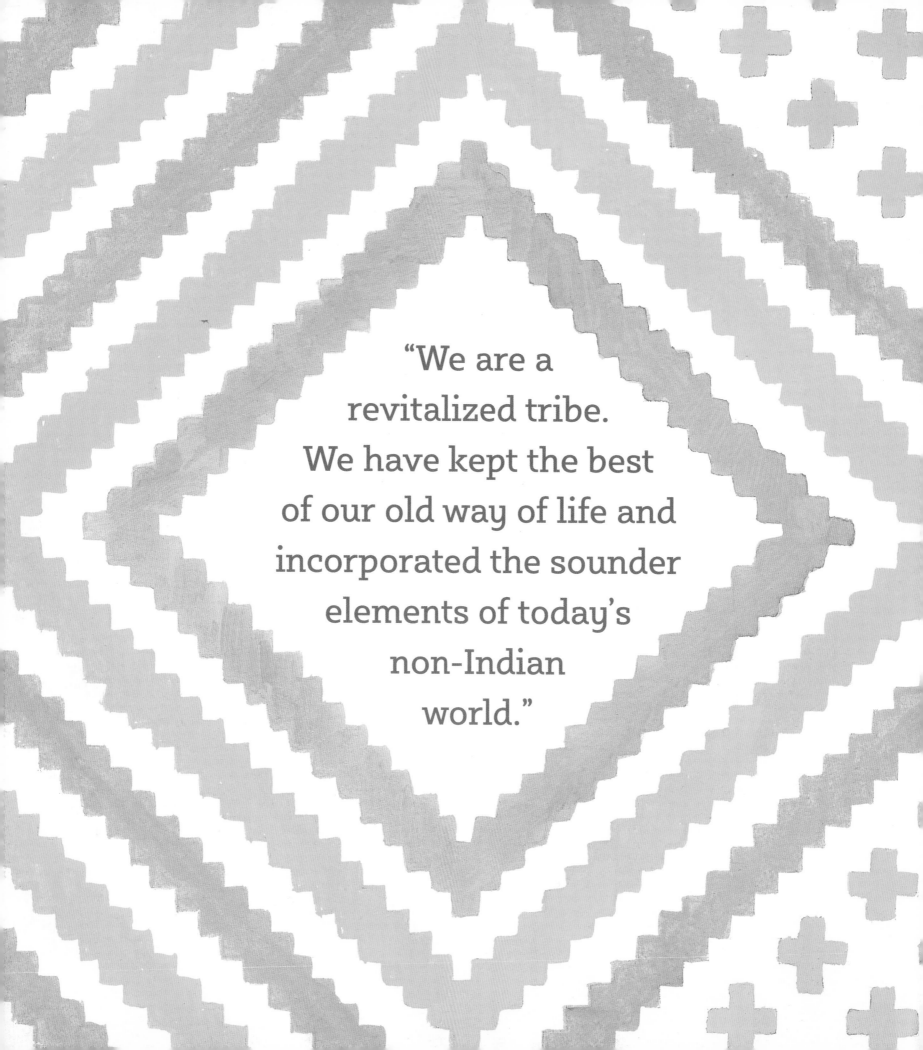

"We are a revitalized tribe. We have kept the best of our old way of life and incorporated the sounder elements of today's non-Indian world."